A Legacy of Leadership: Mentorship and Growth

By Ronald McGinnis Sr

Table of Contents

Acknowledgments: 4
Introduction 6
Chapter 1: The Foundation 10
Chapter 2: Leadership Isn't A Popularity Contest 33
Chapter 3: Being Authentically You 42
Chapter 4: Be The Solution You Want To See 52
Chapter 5: Leading With Grace 59
Chapter 6: Leadership Comes With Challenges 69
Chapter 7: Inspiration and Motivation 79
Chapter 8: All You Need Is A Vision 86
Chapter 9: The Importance of Community 94
Chapter 10: Who Are You When No One Is Looking? 102
Chapter 11: Moments of Reflection 112
Chapter 12: Lessons From an Airman 119
About the Author 125

Copyright©2025 Ronald McGinnis Sr

All rights reserved.

No part of this book can be reproduced in any form without the written permission of the author and its publisher.

All Scripture quotations, unless otherwise indicated, are taken from the King James Version. Copyright© 1982 by Thomas Nelson, Inc Used by permission. All rights reserved.

ISBN: 9798262877119

Acknowledgments:

To my beautiful Bride, Monica, my consultant and adventure partner who is always there for me with prayer, encouragement and love. Thanks for being my "silent" cheerleader in the good and hard times. You are my air, and I love you.

To my daughter, Destanéa, who is such a free spirit and loving leader, you impress me every day. I love you more than Blue Bell kid.

To my daughter, Lydia, you give past your heart to your soul and to see you in action brings me joy. I love you more than Japanese Ramen kid.

To my daughter, Jade, your love and competitive spirit continue to push me to this day. I love you more than Melon soda kid.

To my son, RJ, you are the promise God made to your mother and I and we are forever grateful for you. Your passion to learn is inspiring and dope on so many levels! I love you more than Buc'ees kid.

To my God given son, Derek, you came into our lives with a smile, pure comedy and love. Thanks for choosing to love us too.

To my God given son, David, you came into our lives with a smile, pure love and a willingness to learn. Thanks for choosing to love us too.

To all our family and extended family and friends. Thank you for all the love and support. We wouldn't be here today without your help.

To my Momma and Mema, Yall provided me the structure, strength and love that has propelled me through this life and I am forever grateful to you. I count it a blessing to have been raised by you. I will continue to keep your memories alive as long as I have breath in my lungs.

And to the ONE who is able to keep us from falling. God, I thank you for life, health and strength. You loved me before I knew how to define the feeling with words for myself. Thank you for Jesus, the Holy Spirit, and for your constant provision in all aspects of life.

Introduction

Thank you for picking up my book—it means the world to me. Let me tell you a little about my journey. I come from a small town named Houston, Texas, where I was raised by two extraordinary women: my mother and grandmother. Their strength shaped me, their love grounded me. After high school, I joined the Navy and dedicated 33 years of my life to service. But let me tell you this: those small details, while a part of my story, don't define who I truly am. They only provide a little insight to the person behind the face.

Each one of us carries a story forged not just by where we come from or what we've done, but by the people who've walked beside us, the lessons learned, and the challenges faced. My life, like yours, has been shaped by family, friends, and countless moments of triumph and trials. Our hardships don't define us, but if we look at them through the right perspective we'll realize that they're the sandpaper utilized to smooth out the rough areas.

I believe each experience, every conversation, is a thread that weaves us into the fabric of something greater. The skills I've honed and the knowledge I've gained exist for one purpose: to give back. To uplift, empower, and help someone succeed. And if, in some small way, I've inspired or guided you, then I know I've contributed to making the world a little brighter.

Because here's the truth: change happens, one person at a time. And together, one small act, one shared story at a time, we can leave a legacy of kindness, resilience, and hope.

What makes a great leader? Are leaders born, destined to guide others from the start? Or are they shaped, molded by life's experiences? The truth lies in the harmony of both. Yet, what truly defines a great leader is not solely their origins—it is their ability to inspire. It is the ability to see something in a person that no one else may see, not even themselves. It is the courage to step forward when others hesitate and the gift of igniting the potential in those around them.

In this book, you will uncover the essence of that elusive "it" factor—the driving force that propels leaders to excel. For me, this force is God—a guiding presence that moves us forward and shapes our paths. When we attune ourselves to that still, small voice within, when we remain open to the wisdom in those we meet along life's journey, true transformation becomes inevitable.

True change begins within. It starts with our willingness to grow, to listen, and to act. Only then can we influence the lives of others, creating ripples of positive impact. Change happens one moment, one step, and one person at a time. And the most profound truth? Change is not just a destination—it is a personal journey we must take first.

You might think that changing the world is too ambitious, too lofty a goal—but I urge you to rethink that belief. When you see something that is not right, when you feel that undeniable pull in your heart to make a difference, that moment is the calling. And that responsibility is yours.

The way you bring about change is uniquely yours—it is shaped by your perspective, your experiences, and the impact you are meant to leave behind. But one truth remains: the power to create change is already within you. My purpose in writing this book is to help you uncover that potential. It is to equip you with the tools and the insights that will empower you to become a world-changer in your own remarkable way.

This book is more than words on a page. It is a reflection of my journey—a collection of lessons learned, challenges overcome, and faith that has guided me every step of the way. It is the first of the several volumes I hope to share with you. My prayer is that these pages will not only inspire you but also uplift your spirit and encourage self-reflection. I hope that through my story, you will feel the courage to embrace your own path and create meaningful change in the world around you.

Change does not happen by chance. It starts with intention. It starts with a single moment, a single step, and a single person. And that person is you. Together, let us walk this journey of transformation and leave a lasting legacy of hope and impact.

Chapter 1: The Foundation

Growing up on the northwest side of Houston in Acres Homes—"the 44 (pronounced fo fo)," as we call it—meant being surrounded by a blend of life, energy, and danger, all wrapped together like a relentless tide. To digress for a moment, the name came from city bus route 44 that wound its way through our neighborhood, connecting us to the larger city.

Life in the 44 was never quiet—not like those neighborhoods where the nights are serenaded by crickets or the faint hum of someone's air conditioner. No, here the streets had their own rhythm. The soundtrack of the 44 was sharp, loud, and unapologetically alive. Sirens pierced the air like clockwork—police cars racing through the blocks, ambulances rushing to someone's aid, fire trucks thundering down narrow streets. Those wails were not just sounds; they were reminders of the battles being fought every single day.

As kids, we adapted. Most of us learned to sleep through the chaos. But some nights, the sirens refused to let me drift away. I would lie in bed, staring at the ceiling, counting the minutes between the wails, my young mind spinning with questions. Were those police sirens? An ambulance? A fire truck? What happened? And most hauntingly—who did it happen to?

But here is the thing about growing up in the 44: it teaches you resilience. It builds something in you—a strength, a determination, a drive to rise above and create something better. The sirens that echoed through those nights were not just calls for help; they were calls to action. They reminded me, even as a kid, that life is unpredictable and fragile, but it is also full of opportunity.

The 44 shaped me. It did not define me, but it gave me lessons I carry to this day: that every sound, every moment, has a purpose. That no matter how loud life gets, you can always find your voice and your path within it. And that even in the middle of chaos, there is hope—because every siren is also a sign that someone, somewhere, is trying to make things better. It's just a matter of perspective.

To anyone out there who has ever felt overwhelmed by their environment or trapped by their circumstances, know this: where you come from does not determine where you are going. The 44 may have been tough, but it gave me a foundation to build on—a foundation of grit, faith, and hope. And that, my friends, is what carries us forward.

In the middle of all the noise and chaos, there was my sanctuary—my grandmother's house. It was not far from our home, just a different neighborhood over, but crossing that invisible line felt like stepping into a whole other world. The moment I walked through her door, the weight of the streets seemed to vanish.

It was not just the quiet—although her home did have that blessed stillness that my home could never give me. It was something deeper. Though I could still hear sirens, but I knew that 99% of the time they weren't coming into my grandmother's neighborhood. My grandmother carried this calming presence, this quiet strength that felt like it came from a place beyond the here and now. Her faith was unshakable, a fortress so strong it shielded everything and everyone within its reach. And when I was with her, I felt like nothing outside those walls could touch me.

Every single day, without fail, she prayed and read her Bible in her favorite chair. It did not matter what was happening outside—gunshots cracking the night, sirens wailing, voices shouting in anger or fear. She would sit there, whispering prayers that I knew reached heaven itself. Her words carried weight, not just for me but for everyone in her life. We all knew she had God's ear.

I think about those nights now, the ones where the streets outside felt too heavy to bear. I remember how stepping into my grandmother's home was like finding solid ground in a storm. She taught me that faith is not about ignoring what is happening around you—it is about standing firm in the middle of it. She showed me that peace is not the absence of noise; it is the presence of something greater, something that can quiet your soul even when the world outside is screaming.

Her prayers taught me more than words ever could. They taught me about love, strength, and the unshakable power of faith. And in those moments, sitting beside her while the world roared on, I learned that sanctuaries are not just places—they are people, too.

She prayed for all of us—me, my cousins, the family, our neighbors, even strangers we had never met. It did not matter how dangerous things got outside. It did not matter how many sirens tore through the night, how many times we heard about someone getting hurt or taken away. Inside her house, everything felt different, like the world outside could not reach us.

She would look at me, her voice steady and warm, and say, "God's got you, baby." And somehow, those words reached a place in me nothing else could. It was not that I was naive. We all knew what was out there—the dangers were real, and they were close. But when she said that, it was like the weight of the world shrank just enough for me to breathe again.

Her faith was not just words; it was a shield, an anchor, a light cutting through the darkest nights. We could all feel her faith. When everything around us felt chaotic and uncertain, her prayers and those simple yet powerful words reminded me that there was something bigger at work, something that could hold us steady even when the ground felt like it might crumble beneath our feet.

To this day, I carry her words with me. "God's got you, baby." They are more than a reassurance—they are a promise. A reminder that no matter how loud the sirens, how dark the night, or how uncertain the journey, there is always a peace to be found if we are willing to believe.

There were nights when the air felt heavy, and thick with a kind of tension that made your skin crawl, as if the whole world was holding its breath. Maybe it was the distant echo of shouting from a few streets over, or the shadowy figures of men gathered on the corner, speaking in hushed, urgent tones. Whatever it was, those moments carried a weight that even a child could feel—a warning that something bad might be just around the corner.

But even then, my grandmother's prayers were a fortress. They wrapped around me like an invisible shield, making me feel like nothing could get to us. Her faith had this way of cutting through the darkness, of quieting the fear that lurked at the edges of my little world. While the streets outside seemed to pulse with violence and danger, her house became the safest place I could imagine.

I would lie awake some nights, hearing the muffled chaos of the world outside—the shouting, the sirens, the heavy silence that came between—but none of it could touch 6-

year-old me. Inside her home, inside the sanctuary of her faith, I was untouchable. Her prayers, whispered in that steady, calming voice, were more powerful than anything the streets could throw at us.

My grandmother's belief was not just a comfort; it was a promise, a reminder that even when the world feels heavy and uncertain, there is a place of safety, of love, of unshakable peace. For me, that place was wherever she was. And even now, I carry that faith with me, that sense of protection, knowing that the power of her prayers continues to shield me, no matter where I go.

Looking back now, I see that those sirens were not just background noise—they were threads woven into the fabric of my life. They were constant reminders of the dangers we faced daily, simply because of where we lived. Each wail told a story, echoing the challenges of a neighborhood where survival often felt like a victory in itself.

And yet, those same sirens also gave contrast to something much greater—the sanctuary of my grandmother's house. The peace I felt there was not because the world outside had suddenly become less dangerous. No, the streets were just as chaotic, just as unforgiving. But what made the difference was her. Her love, her unwavering faith—it was as if they formed an invisible barrier that nothing from the outside could penetrate.

Her presence made me believe in safety, even in a world that seemed determined to convince me otherwise. It was not just the quiet of her home; it was the strength that radiated from her. Her prayers, her steady reassurance—they were more powerful than any chaos the streets could conjure. Now she would not only provide prayer and scriptures but tangible words the older I got, like: "Ronald, ain't no need to be out past 10 or 11 o'clock at night because ain't nothing open but thighs and bars." To which my only retort was, "Yes ma'am."

In those moments, I realized that peace is not about silencing the noise around you; it is about finding something louder within you. My grandmother gave me that. Her love and her faith were like an anchor, grounding me even when the world felt like it was spinning out of control. To this day, I carry the memory of that peace with me, a reminder that no matter where life takes me, there is always a refuge to be found in faith, in love, and in the strength passed down by those who believe in something greater.

Her home was more than just a house; it was a sanctuary—a refuge where faith and love stood unwavering against whatever the night brought our way. No matter how chaotic the world outside became, her home was a fortress where the noise of the streets could not penetrate, and the weight of fear lifted.

Even now, when I hear sirens, I think of her. I think of that quiet, unshakable strength she carried, a strength that seemed effortless but was born from a faith so profound it could move mountains. She shared that strength with me, passing it on in ways that were as subtle as they were life-changing.

I did not just survive those years because of her—I thrived. She gave me more than protection; she gave me a foundation. Growing up, I carried a sense of safety that went far beyond the walls of her house. It was a security rooted in love, in prayer, laughter and in the kind of faith that wraps itself around you like a warm, unyielding embrace.

When I left for the Navy at 19, I carried that with me. It was in every prayer she whispered, every reassuring word she spoke, and every ounce of belief she poured into me. Her love and her faith shaped the person I became, giving me the courage to step into the unknown, knowing that no matter where life took me, I would always carry the refuge she built in my heart.

Growing up in "the 44" was about so much more than just surviving. Sure, danger was always around the corner—you learned early on to keep your head on a swivel and stay out of trouble—but there was a kind of beauty to it too, a vibrance that made the 44 unforgettable. It was a place where love and laughter lived side by side with the chaos. Community thrived, even in the hardest of times, and you always knew someone had your back.

Take my best friend Mark's mom, Momma Wilson. She was a force of nature, a true prayer warrior just like my grandmother, and she watched over us like a hawk. It didn't matter whose kid you were—if you were in her orbit, she was looking out for you, praying for you, making sure you stayed on the right path. Then there was our other best friend Eric, who stayed with his grandparents and uncle.

They were the kind of family who didn't just take care of Eric; they looked after all of us, keeping us in line when we needed it most.

It was like we were all one big family, stitched together by faith, love, and that unspoken code of community. Those bonds made the 44 more than just a neighborhood—they made it a home. And even now, when I think about it, I don't just remember the danger; I remember the laughter. The porch conversations. The sound of kids running down the street, carefree, for just a moment.

The 44 taught me resilience, but it also showed me the beauty of togetherness. It was a place where tough love met endless compassion, where people like Momma Wilson and Eric's family gave us the guidance and strength to thrive. And no matter where life takes me, I'll always carry the lessons and love of that community with me.

Momma Wilson had a way about her. She could quote scripture at the drop of a hat, but it was never just words—she had this gift of bringing it down to our level, making sure we not only heard it, but felt it. Whether we were ready for it or not, she was determined to sprinkle a little bit of the Word into our lives.

I'll never forget the night I spent over at Mark's house when his sister, Shondra, decided we should watch *The Omen*. She wanted to watch it, so we all went along with it. We couldn't have been more than 10 or 11 years old, just kids trying to act tougher than we really were. Now, let me tell you—I'm not built for scary movies. Never have been, never will be. But back then, I wasn't about to let them know that. No way was I going to look weak in front of Mark and Shondra. So, I sat through it.

From the very first eerie scene, I was on edge. Every shadow, every creepy moment had me gripping whatever was closest to me, but I kept my face as straight as I could. By the time the credits rolled, though, I was done for. My fear bubbled over, and I couldn't hold it in anymore. I started crying—real tears, the kind you can't stop once they start—and blurted out, "I'm going to Hell! The devil's gonna kill me!"

Looking back, it's funny now, but in that moment, it was real. That movie had shaken me to my core. And you can bet that the next morning, Momma Wilson wasn't going to let me leave her house without some spiritual reassurance. She probably saw right through me and had one of her scripture-laden pep talks ready, making sure I left with a little extra armor on my soul.

Momma Wilson wasn't just about correcting us with the Word; she was about reminding us of grace, of love, and of the fact that God's got us—even when the scary stuff of life makes us believe otherwise.

Shondra and Momma Wilson tried their best to calm me down, but it was no use. Shondra was laughing so hard she could barely breathe, which only made things worse for me. I wasn't hearing any of it. Through tears, I blurted out, "Y'all don't understand! Y'all know God, but I don't!"

Now, looking back, it is funny—hilarious, even. Honestly, even in that moment, there was probably something a little funny about it. But I wasn't laughing then. I was dead serious. That fear, that raw emotion—it was real. It wasn't just the movie; it was the idea that I didn't know God like they did. To my 10- or 11-year-old self, it felt like I was on the outside of this protective circle they had through their faith.

That night, for the first time, I realized the power of faith—not just as something comforting, but as something that could feel like a shield, a safe place to stand when the rest of the world felt scary. Shondra and Momma Wilson had that, and I could see it. I could feel it. And more than anything, I wanted it too.

Looking back, I laugh at the drama of that moment, but I'm also grateful for it. It was a turning point for me, one of those moments that stays with you, shaping the way you think about life and faith. It taught me that fear doesn't have to have the last word, and it showed me that God's love is not about being "inside" or "outside" a circle. It is there for all of us, waiting, even when we don't know it yet.

What I didn't realize at the time was that moment—scary as it was—planted a seed in me. That fear of not having a relationship with Jesus stayed with me, lingering in my thoughts long after the night ended. It wasn't just about being terrified of the devil or worrying about going to Hell. It was deeper than that. It was about recognizing that there was something bigger out there, something vast and powerful that I didn't yet understand, but deeply wanted to.

Looking back, I see how that night marked the beginning of my journey towards faith. It was the spark that ignited a curiosity, a yearning to know the God that I had seen my grandmother and Momma Wilson turn to with such certainty. Their faith wasn't just words or rituals—it was alive, present, and undeniable. Even in my fear, I could feel the pull of that kind of connection, that kind of assurance.

That night showed me something crucial: faith is a journey, and every journey starts somewhere. For me, it started with a moment of fear that opened my heart to the possibility of something greater. I didn't know it then, but that seed was planted, and over time, it began to grow. That growth changed my life, giving me a foundation I didn't even know I needed.

Life does have a way of surprising us, doesn't it? Moments that seem ordinary—like a childhood sleepover—can turn into something far more profound. That night in Mark's living room, what started as fear sparked something greater inside of me. It may not have felt like it at the time, but that small, deeply human moment planted a seed that would grow into a lifelong journey.

Faith often begins like that—a nudge, a whisper, a stirring you cannot quite shake. It is not always found all at once; sometimes it takes time, patience, and a little wandering. But what matters is that the seed was planted, and it stayed with you, drawing you toward something bigger than yourself.

The beauty of your story is in how that moment of fear transformed into a search for faith, a quest that ultimately shaped the person you are today. Gratitude for that process—for the ways life leads us, even through unexpected and uncomfortable moments—is such a powerful testament to growth.

Your journey reminds us all that faith is not about having every answer; it is about seeking, learning, and opening our hearts to something greater. Thank you for sharing that part of your story—it's inspiring in the most authentic way.

One day after school when we heard that a neighbor at the far end of the street had been shot and killed by his wife. Driven by a mix of curiosity and shock, we wanted to go see what had happened. By the time we arrived, the body was gone, along with the police and emergency responders, leaving only the buzz of the neighborhood talking about what took place.

Another thing that remained, however, was a lot of blood in their neighbor's driveway—a sight unlike anything we had ever seen. It was overwhelming, both the sheer amount and the harsh reality that it all could end up there, spilled across the concrete. Sights like that don't leave you, but they do remind you of how quickly and brutally life could change in an instant. This was our first visual of that harsh reality that our parents had told us our entire short lives.

Now please don't get the wrong idea—I had a great upbringing, full of fun, adventure, and more memories than I can count. Sure, we grew up in a tough neighborhood without a lot of money, but that didn't stop us from making the most of every day. One of our favorite pastimes was exploring the woods behind our homes. Those woods were like a different world to us. We'd go out there searching for wild berries, picking handfuls to snack on, but always keeping a careful eye out for snakes. We weren't scared of much, but we knew better than to mess with a snake if we saw one slithering through the brush. On the other side of the street, behind those homes was a bayou that ran all the way behind those houses. We'd go in there when it was low looking for crawfish and turtles, for no other reason than to mess with them.

Then there were the games. We had an unofficial neighborhood basketball court in Mark's backyard, and we'd play until the sun started to set, drenched in sweat and laughter. Touch/tackle football in the street and in the neighbor's yards was another favorite, and we had to be just as watchful as we were competitive. Anytime a car came down the road because at the time there were no speed bumps. So, someone would shout, "Car time!" and we'd scatter to the side, waiting until the street was clear to start up again. It was a rhythm we were all used to—playing, laughing, pausing for cars, and then diving back into the game as if nothing had happened.

On one occasion we were playing in the neighbor's yard with a ball and it got away from one of the girls. She ran after it and a car hit her and ran completely over her. She got up and walked to the opposite side of the street and collapsed. She didn't hear the screams from everyone to stop, she just went after what she was focused on. Thankfully some of the men that were looking jumped in front of the car and stopped it because the driver tried to keep going. The results of this and other near misses prompted the city to put speed bumps in. No one was ever hit or had a close call again.

I had a lot of fun as a kid, and I wouldn't trade those memories for anything. But one of the things that stands out most from my childhood wasn't the games or the adventures—it was going to the Union Hall downtown with my mom. She worked for Southwestern Bell and was deeply involved in the union. I didn't understand all the ins and outs of what they did at the time, but I knew it was important. Watching her in action at the Union Hall was something that filled me with pride. She wasn't just my mom; she was a leader, a force to be reckoned with among her peers, and seeing her in that light changed the way I saw her.

There was something about the way she carried herself in those meetings. She wasn't loud, but she had a quiet strength, and people listened when she spoke. I could tell that she commanded respect without even trying. It astounded me, honestly, to see her like that—so sure of herself, so confident. Watching her interact with other members of the union, I realized that leadership wasn't just about having power; it was about earning people's trust, respect and being someone they could rely on. I was young, but those moments left a lasting impression on me.

Without even knowing it, my mom was teaching me my first lessons on how to be a great leader. She didn't sit me down and explain it step by step; I just learned by watching her. She showed me that leadership isn't about being the loudest in the room, but about having integrity, standing up for what's right, and always having the backs of the people who depend on you. Those lessons have stayed with me throughout my life, shaping the way I approach challenges and how I treat others.

Looking back, I realize now that my environment was shaping me to be a leader long before I ever set foot in the Navy. The experiences I had, from navigating the challenges of growing up in the 44 to watching my mother at the Union Hall, all played a part in molding me. Without even knowing it, I was absorbing lessons on resilience, teamwork, and standing up for others. When I eventually enlisted, I took everything I'd learned—whether from my family, the streets, the basketball courts, or football fields—and applied it in a way that allowed me to help others, no matter where they came from or what challenges they faced. I didn't just want to lead; I wanted to serve and uplift those around me.

What's funny is that the Navy wasn't even on my radar until my senior year of high school. Growing up, the only military branch I had any real knowledge of was the Army, and even that was limited. I had a cousin I'd never met who was stationed in Germany, and people in my family always talked about him like he was doing something amazing. But beyond that, I didn't know much about the military. I always got pretty good grades, but I like many others saw sports as a primary way out, hence my plan to earn a football scholarship. The coaching staff at my high school was phenomenal so that became my focus—until life threw a couple curveballs my way, and suddenly, my path took an unexpected turn.

Basketball, though, was my real passion. I loved the game, and I was good at it. But being 5'10" on a good day meant my NBA dreams were just that—dreams. It wasn't something that was likely to happen, not in the era I was coming up in. Still, the game taught me so much: how to work as a team, how to lead, how to stay disciplined, and how to handle both victory and defeat. These were lessons that stuck with me long after I stopped playing competitively. In many ways, watching my mom and playing basketball prepared me for life in the Navy. It taught me to push through pain and challenges, to lead by example, and to always find a way to contribute, even if I wasn't the tallest or the strongest player on the court.

Every experience we have, whether good or bad, holds a lesson. If we take time to pray and ask God about the purpose behind each moment, we can uncover the object lessons intended for us. God is always speaking and teaching, but are we listening and ready to receive those lessons with a spiritual "pen and pad" in hand? By focusing on the lesson rather than the negative aspects of an experience, we shift our mindset from one of defeat to growth. This doesn't mean we should ignore the hard moments or pretend they don't have an impact on us but acknowledging them is part of the journey.

Once we've acknowledged what happened, the decision is on us. We must choose to move forward. Dwelling on problems won't stop time or change the past. Life won't slow down for us, so we must be intentional about not letting setbacks keep us from an amazing comeback. Embracing this approach means actively seeking and deciding that growth in every moment is your only option. With each lesson, we strengthen our resilience and deepen our spiritual awareness, allowing God's guidance to shape us for what lies ahead. All these experiences helped develop my foundation.

What is your foundation made of and based on?

Chapter 2: Leadership Isn't A Popularity Contest

When I left for the Navy, I remember the tight embrace from my mom and Mema, their arms wrapped around me like they were trying to hold on to every last bit of me before I went off into the unknown. It was the kind of hug that said a thousand things without a word. I didn't know it then, but that moment would replay in my mind many times in the years to come, and it still does today. It expressed the deep love and support I'd always received from them. After that, I left with the Recruiter and headed to the hotel where I'd spend the night before going to MEPS for processing the next morning. Little did I know my mom and one of my aunts would show up that morning to support me raising my right hand to swear into the Navy. Sometimes I look at the photo someone captured for us and tears come to my eyes as well as a smile. That was a special moment.

But, that previous night in the hotel was the first time I had ever stayed in one and I was alone. The quiet felt almost unsettling, and I could hardly sleep because it was so foreign to me. Growing up, there was always noise—sirens echoing through the neighborhood, music playing in the background, or the steady hum of life in Acres Homes. My mom loved music, especially that classic Motown sound. If it wasn't Marvin Gaye or Smokey Robinson on the record player, it was Stevie Wonder or The Temptations. I remember the day Marvin Gaye died like it was yesterday. My mom cried like she had lost a close family member. I mean, I knew he was good, but dang, my mom was inconsolable for a couple days.

Music wasn't just entertainment in our house—it was woven into the fabric of the McGinnis family's lives. Everyone sang, especially in church, and when I say they sang, I mean they *sang*. There was no half-stepping in any of the churches we were members of and choir members. Voices in my family weren't just good—they were powerful. Music brought us together, just like church did and the board and card games we often played during family get togethers. Growing up in that environment gave us a solid foundation. My Mema would tell me stories about her parents, Big Daddy, and Big Mama, and how they built our family up from nothing. They worked hard, and through their faith and perseverance, they gave us a strong name. Those stories gave me a deep sense of pride, even as a little kid. I knew from the time I was six that I had a responsibility to carry on that legacy, and more than that, I wanted to take it to another level. I wasn't about to let my ancestors down, and my mindset still hasn't changed in that regard.

Things around our home started to change when I reached middle school. In the middle of the school year, my mom moved us across town to be closer to her job. I didn't want to leave the only home I had known, and certainly not my family or the friends I had grown up with since I was six. It felt like my world was being pulled out from under me, and I was angry about it. But what could I do? I had no choice in the matter. I just had to go with the flow, even if I didn't like it.

For the next two years, I played football, basketball, and ran track. I did well in all of them, but my heart was always back in the 44. No matter how many new friends I made or how much fun I had, it never really felt like home. I kept a bit of distance between myself and my new environment, like I was just waiting for the day I could go back to where I really belonged.

At my new school, I didn't talk to many people at first. In fact, I didn't really talk to anyone. I spent the rest of that school year keeping to myself, still holding on to the resentment of being uprooted. But something shifted after that summer break. When we came back for seventh grade, I decided to play football for the school, and that's when things started to change. I began making friends, and before I knew it, I was part of the "in" crowd, one of the so-called "popular" kids. But I didn't really understand what that meant because, in my mind, I was just Ronald—just the same kid from the 44 who loved sports and making people laugh.

During that summer, I barely spoke to my mom. I had an attitude, and I was mad that she had moved us without asking me. I felt like she had taken me away from everything I knew and loved, and I didn't know how to handle that. I was just a kid trying to make sense of things that were out of my control. I'll never forget one Saturday morning when she told me to get in the car. I asked her where we were going, and she hit me with the classic "don't question grown folks, just ride." I didn't have much of a choice, so I got in. We drove to what looked like a strip mall, and I followed her into a taekwondo dojo. I was confused. I had no idea why we were there until we were called into what I assumed was the owner's office. My mom started talking to the man, explaining that I had an attitude problem and a quick temper. I was shocked. I couldn't believe she was putting me on blast like that. I sat there thinking, "I know she didn't just tell this man my business." But then the man, who I would later know as Sensei, looked straight at me—not at my mom—and in the calmest, yet somehow scariest voice ever, said, "Don't worry, ma'am. We'll fix that."

For the next six months, I went to taekwondo regularly. At first, I hated every minute of it. I didn't want to be there, and I definitely didn't want some Asian man I could barely understand trying to "fix" me. But slowly, something started to change. I began to respect him. Sensei wasn't just teaching me how to fight; he was teaching me discipline, patience, and control. Critical things I needed to be a man. Though I didn't realize it at the time, but he was helping me channel all that anger and frustration into something positive.

As time went on, I also began to see my mom in a different light. I started to understand why she had moved us. She wasn't trying to punish me or take me away from my friends;

she was trying to put me in an environment where I could grow, where I could gain a new perspective. She knew that I needed to learn how to adapt and overcome, not just in our old neighborhood but in the wider world. In my old neighborhood I was surrounded by primarily blacks, but she wanted to expose me to way more. She understood the kind of world I was coming up in and she was trying to prepare me the best way she knew how.

Moving from a predominantly Black school to a predominantly white one was a culture shock, no doubt about it. But I adapted. I learned to navigate this new space and found my footing. My mom would often remind me, "Ronald, there's more to life than where we come from. Keep your mind open to new things, people and perspectives." At the time, I didn't fully appreciate those words, but they stuck with me. They were seeds that would later grow and bloom when I joined the Navy.

In hindsight, all of those experiences—moving to a new school, learning martial arts, being pushed out of my comfort zone—were preparing me for something bigger. They were laying the groundwork for the next chapter of my life, even though I couldn't see it at the time. Every lesson I learned, every challenge I faced, would serve me well when I finally stepped into the unknown and embarked on my journey in the Navy.

It all began with my mom's decision to move us across town, a choice that wasn't popular with anyone, including me. At the time, I was too wrapped up in my own anger and frustration to understand the weight of what she was doing. It wasn't just about uprooting our lives; it was about positioning us for something better, something she saw that no one else did. Looking back, I realize that her decision wasn't just difficult—it was courageous. She didn't care that no one agreed with her. She had a vision, and she was determined to follow through.

As the years went on, I came to understand just how much that move shaped me. It taught me about adaptability, resilience, and the importance of stepping outside your comfort zone. More than that, it showed me the strength it takes to make tough decisions, even when those decisions might make you unpopular. My mom's willingness to stand firm in her choice, even when everyone doubted her, planted a seed in me. I didn't realize it at the time, but that lesson would become one of the cornerstones of how I approached challenges in my own life.

Watching my mom taught me the importance of inner strength and resilience. Regardless of who's watching or cheering, the drive to keep going has to come from within. Life is full of moments where the support we hope for may not always be there, but we must have an unwavering commitment to push forward.

Not everyone will agree with our decisions, and that's okay. Part of growing is learning that not every choice we make will be popular or even understood by others. Yet, when we make a decision, it's crucial to live with it and embrace it. If it was wrong, then we learn and if it was right someone that doubted you learned. In either case it's a win. It's all a matter of perspective. This inner resolve, much like what I witnessed in my mom, is what carries us through challenges and helps us stand firm in our beliefs and actions.

Her thought process—her clarity, decisiveness, and unwavering belief that she was doing the right thing—still resonates with me today. Every major decision I've faced, whether in the Navy or in life, has been guided by the memory of her strength during that time. I often ask myself, "What would my Momma do or say in this situation?" That question has helped me navigate some of the toughest moments of my life, reminding me that sometimes you have to make the hard call, even when no one else understands. Even when those closest to you don't agree.

In many ways, her decision to move us wasn't just about changing our physical location—it was about setting the tone for the way I would live my life while simultaneously shifting my perspective. It taught me that sometimes you can't just walk around the corner or up the street for advice. You have to work it out on your own and live with the consequences of your decision. She showed me what it means to lead, not just by words, but by actions. Now, when I face choices that seem impossible or when I feel the weight of uncertainty, I think of her, and I know that if she could make that leap as one of the few black women in her position, then so can I.

Are your decisions predicated off other's thoughts of you or your drive to do what's right?

Chapter 3: Being Authentically You

My first ship, the USS San Jose, was more than just a vessel, it was a place where I quickly learned that if you didn't take the time to develop your character, you would fall in line with the crowd. And believe me, I saw plenty of Sailors fall victim to this. They wanted to be in the "in" crowd so badly that they were willing to compromise who they were. They would act like they were someone they really weren't just to fit in, but that wasn't me. I wasn't raised to follow the crowd, and I wasn't about to start now. My mom would often say, "Show me your friends and I will know who you really are."

Even back home, I didn't let peer pressure get to me. Sometimes my friends would question why I was heading home as soon as the streetlights started coming on, knowing full well that my mom wasn't home. My answer was always the same, five simple words: "Because my momma said so." That foundation, listening to my mom and respecting her rules carried over to my Navy life. It was a compass I could trust, even when I was far from home.

One thing did follow me from home, though, my temper. I had worked hard to tame it over the years, but it was still there, simmering beneath the surface. On the ship, they called me "Quick," a nickname that stuck, probably because it reminded them of Eddie Murphy's character in *Harlem Nights*. It wasn't just about my temper, though. It was about my quick wit and sharp tongue as well. I'd learned to control my mouth, too, but it took a lot of effort. That control didn't just come from Sensei and his teachings; I'd learned it by watching my mom and other leaders I respected.

Those lessons in self-discipline proved to be crucial. In the Navy, tempers flare in high-stress situations, and if you couldn't control yours, you wouldn't last long. I knew I had to keep mine in check if I wanted to be successful because getting kicked out the Navy and going home with that embarrassment wasn't an option.

One of the most important things I did when I first arrived on the USS San Jose was take the time to study the Navy's regulations and the people around me. I read everything I could get my hands on. Rules about conduct, discipline, and, most importantly, how I was supposed to be treated. I wasn't just some wide-eyed Sailor. I wanted to truly understand my rights, especially when it came to things like equal opportunity.

The ship had some serious racial issues, and I saw the discrepancies in how non-white Sailors were treated compared to their white counterparts. It was blatant and unsettling. I knew I couldn't change the system overnight, but I could make sure that I was equipped with knowledge. As a young man, at first I blamed the Navy, but I came to realize because of one senior Sailor that it's not the Navy that supports racism, but some of the people. So I learned how to carry myself in front of those certain people and what to say, and I started keeping a journal of the injustices I witnessed.

The racial issues on the ship were something I could never have anticipated. There were clear contradictions in how Sailors were punished depending on their skin color. It didn't sit right with me, and I wasn't about to just accept it. I started keeping detailed notes of the incidents I saw, like a lawyer building a case. I knew I had to protect myself, and I knew that knowledge and understanding of the Navy's policies and procedures was the best weapon I could hold.

There were days when I felt like I wanted to quit and not re-enlist, and I wasn't alone. There were other Sailors who felt the same way. We stuck together, but more than that, I relied on the character I had been developing since childhood. It gave me the strength to stand tall, even when things felt unfair. One of the biggest failures most people fall victim to is giving up right before they see and experience a breakthrough.

Character is something that comes from within, and it doesn't change overnight. It's built over time, through challenges, setbacks, and moments where you have to decide whether you'll stand up for what's right or follow the crowd. I knew from my upbringing that following the crowd wasn't an option my family would approve of, and the Navy only reinforced that.

The more I watched people around me fall into toxic patterns, the more determined I became to develop myself, and get more rank so that my voice would be heard and get to a position to help make changes for Sailors coming behind me. I wanted to be someone others could respect, and not because I was perfect, but because I had integrity. And that integrity, that moral compass, became my shield against the challenges I faced.

I realized early on that developing character wasn't something you could do alone. You need accountability partners, people who aren't afraid to tell you the truth when you're veering off course. For me, that accountability came from my prayers, my study of the Bible and people I trusted to tell me the truth. My faith became a cornerstone for my personal growth, helping me see the areas where I needed to improve and giving me the strength to work on them.

I wasn't content with being a "good person." I wanted to be someone with a strong moral foundation, someone who made a difference in the lives of others. That required real work, coupled with constant, intentional work on myself. If there's one thing I've learned, it's that self-reflection is key to personal growth. You have to be willing to look in the mirror and take a hard look at who you are. If the person staring back at you is just "okay," then there's still work to be done. I wanted to look in the mirror and love who I saw. I wanted to be proud of the person I was becoming, and that meant being honest with myself about where I needed to improve. It wasn't easy. Growth never is. But I knew that if

I could develop my character and maintain my integrity, I would be able to handle whatever challenges came my way.

I wasn't content with simply being a "good person." I aspired to be someone with a deeper moral foundation, someone who truly made a difference in the lives of others. That vision required more than just surface-level goodness; it demanded a commitment to meaningful self-work. I realized early on that if I wanted to reach that goal, I would need to face some uncomfortable truths about myself with constant looks at the man in the mirror. Growing into a person of integrity wouldn't happen overnight, nor would it be easy. But I felt compelled to rise above complacency and strive for something greater. To truly transform, I needed to dig deep.

Self-reflection became an essential part of daily life along the journey. It's one thing to feel like you're doing alright, but it's another to recognize and confront the parts of yourself that still need work and then commit to doing the work. Growth requires honesty, and honesty isn't always comfortable. It's humbling to admit that you're not the person you want to be yet. But if I couldn't be honest with myself, how could I expect to grow? To me, seeing the areas

I needed to improve was a sign that I cared enough about me and my effect on others to change.

There were days when this process felt overwhelming. Growth, after all, is a continuous climb. For every step forward, there were moments of doubt, fatigue, and sometimes even failure. But I reminded myself of the scripture that highlights that even a just man falls. I reminded myself that each setback was also an opportunity to become more resilient. I had to learn that personal development wasn't about perfection but persistence. Which is hard for a person like me who is a perfectionist. With each hurdle, I became a little stronger, a little wiser, and more equipped to handle the complexities of life. I didn't just want to be someone who stood by their values when times were easy; I wanted to be someone who stayed true when things got tough.

Loving who I saw in the mirror became a goal I worked toward each day. It wasn't about achieving an end point, where I could suddenly declare myself "complete." Instead, it was about feeling pride in my progress and the person I was becoming. I didn't just want to like myself; I wanted to be proud of myself. To reach that place, I had to be relentless in examining my actions, intentions, and beliefs. Though challenging, it was the only way I could continue to grow with purpose. With each new challenge came new insight into another area to grow.

There aren't any shortcuts to becoming the person you envision. It's a daily commitment, to the journey. The rewards of this path—the strength, the self-respect, the peace of knowing I was living authentically—were well worth the effort. Growth may never be easy, but the sense of purpose and pride that comes with it have made every step worthwhile. And in the end, that's what drives me to keep pushing forward.

One of the most important lessons I learned in the Navy, and in life, was the importance of giving yourself grace. Personal growth takes time. It takes patience. And most of all, it takes an understanding that you're not going to get it right every day. There were times when I stumbled, times when my temper got the best of me or I said something I shouldn't have. But instead of beating myself up, I learned to apologize, give myself grace and keep moving forward. Each day was a new opportunity to be better, to learn from my mistakes, and to keep developing into the person I wanted to be.

The Navy challenged me in ways I couldn't have imagined, but it also gave me the opportunity to strengthen my resolve. I had to decide who I wanted to be, and then I had to stand firm in that decision. There were plenty of opportunities to stray from the path, to compromise my character for the sake of fitting in. But like I said before, that wasn't an option because I could hear my mom's and many family members voices saying that's not what McGinnis's do.

I had seen too many people follow the crowd and lose themselves and their careers in the process. That wasn't going to be my story. I had too much at stake. My legacy, my integrity, and the respect of the people who mattered most to me. I wasn't willing to loose any of that.

One of the most powerful things I learned during this time was the importance of leading by example. People watch what you do more than just listening to what you say. If you want to be a leader, you have to be someone others can not only look up to but be the person others are willing to and really want to follow, someone whose actions align with their words. I wasn't perfect, but I tried to lead in a way that showed others what was possible. I wanted to be the kind of person who inspired others to be the very best version of themselves. So, I leave you with three words to end this chapter. Do the work!

Chapter 4: Be The Solution You Want To See

Leadership is more than just giving orders and enforcing rules. It's about understanding people, building relationships, and creating an environment where your team not only thrives, but trusts you enough to follow you into challenging situations. I came from an impoverished area where leadership wasn't handed to anyone; you had to earn it. My background forced me to understand early on that I had to rise above my circumstances, and that meant constantly working on myself, understanding my flaws, and capitalizing on my strengths. That doesn't mean I didn't at times have fear and doubt, but that I was willing to fight through those emotions because I kept my goal in sight.

When I got to the Navy, I saw that leadership wasn't too different from what I learned back home. Just like in the streets, you couldn't fake being a leader. People knew when you were pretending. I watched leaders who didn't have the trust of their Sailors struggle to get things done. Those who led with arrogance or a lack of empathy were quickly found out. You can only fake authenticity for so long. But the ones who had credibility and character, those were the leaders people respected, even in the toughest times.

Leadership, I learned, was earned by showing up consistently, by being the one who knew the job and the people. It wasn't just about leading during the calm but keeping your composure during the storm. That was something I had to internalize deeply, especially when I saw Sailors looking at me for directions when situations got tense. And trust me, there were plenty of tense situations. But you earn that trust by proving day in and day out that you're capable of making decisions with the welfare of your team in mind. They become your family away from family and you don't let family down. You show up!

When you come from a background like mine, you learn to work hard and make things happen despite the obstacles. That resilience and ingenuity helped shape my leadership style. I understood that many of the people I led had their own struggles, so I led with empathy, knowing that some of the men and women in uniform had traveled the same hard road I had. But I also held them accountable because I knew, as they did, that no one was going to do the work for them and that through that work they would be their own best advocates.

What I tried to instill in my Sailors was the idea that leadership was a process, not a position. It required constant reflection, discipline, and growth. Every experience, whether it was a successful mission or a personal challenge, was an opportunity to sharpen your leadership skills. We all come from different backgrounds, but what connected us was the commitment to rise up together, each of us working to be better than we were the day before.

Character is everything in the Navy, and it's everything in life. In the military, your character determines not only how people see you but also how much responsibility they're willing to give you. It determines if you're willing to charge into a dangerous situation or stand by while others do it. It was drilled into me early on that in a place like the Navy, you could be highly skilled, but if you lacked integrity or accountability, you wouldn't last long. This principle became my mantra as I rose through the ranks.

Coming from an area in Houston where resources were limited, where people often had to make do with what little they had, you learn a lot about character. I grew up watching people cut corners, and seeing others give up because life had beaten them down. But I also saw examples of resilience and people holding onto their dignity no matter how tough things got. I chose to be part of that latter group. And when I joined the Navy, that decision helped me rise above the challenges I faced.

Character isn't something that just shows up when you're promoted or given more responsibility. It's developed in the small decisions you make every day. Whether you're on a ship in the middle of the ocean or back home in a tough neighborhood, your word is all you have. In the Navy, I quickly realized that people respected those who were consistent. If you said you'd do something, you had to follow through. If you made a mistake, you had to own it. And if you wanted to lead others, you had to first lead yourself with integrity and intestinal fortitude.

Building character is a lifelong process. I'm still doing the work on myself because I know that the journey doesn't end. There's always another level of growth, another test that reveals something else you need to work on. I thanked and thanked God for those times and situations. For me, they mean I need to continuously check myself and hold myself to a higher standard than anyone else ever could. I wasn't just trying to rise up for the sake of rising, I was doing it because I knew that real success starts within.

A crucial step in refining your character is understanding who you are at your deepest level. It's not just about the roles you play or the accomplishments you've earned. Those are nice, but at the end of the day they shouldn't define you, but it's your core values and beliefs that define you. To truly evolve, you have to take a step back and assess what drives you when no one is watching. This level of self-awareness is essential because it serves as the foundation for lasting change. If you don't know who you are fundamentally, any changes you make will be superficial and short-lived.

Once you have a clear understanding of your inner self, the next question is: why are you seeking change? Your motivation needs to go beyond surface-level desires like wanting more success or admiration. It must be rooted in a deeper, more meaningful reason. Perhaps it's spiritual, perhaps it's about aligning your life with your values, breaking negative patterns, or becoming a better version of yourself for those you care about. When you identify a strong, non-superficial reason for changing, it gives you the perseverance to stay committed, even when things get tough.

Another important aspect to consider is who benefits from your growth aside from yourself. Personal development isn't just about your own well-being; it has a ripple effect on the people around you. If you become a more patient, empathetic, or disciplined person, your relationships will improve, your leadership will strengthen, and your contributions to your community and society as a whole will grow. It's equally important to recognize that your growth doesn't happen in isolation, and that it impacts everyone you interact with. This realization can be a powerful motivator.

Additionally, thinking beyond yourself forces you to be accountable. When you know that others are relying on you to be the best version of yourself, it adds weight to your personal development journey. It's no longer just about self-improvement for its own sake but about being in a position to uplift and support others. Whether it's family, friends, coworkers, or your community, your growth can inspire and influence those around you to pursue their own journey of character refinement.

In the end, refining your character is about connecting your internal growth to a greater purpose, and realizing that it's not always about you alone. Society today is very self-focused, but it's really important about understanding who you are, why you want to change, and how your growth positively impacts the world beyond you. When you approach personal development with this mindset, it becomes a transformative process that goes far deeper than superficial adjustments. It becomes a lifelong journey of evolving into someone who not only benefits from their growth but also leaves a lasting impact on others.

What's your vehicle for change and growth? Mine is God.

Chapter 5: Leading With Grace

I experienced a lot in my two years onboard the USS San Jose that shaped me into who I am today. The ship's environment was full of challenges, both professional and personal, and I could have easily allowed it to jade me, but I wouldn't be a McGinnis if I succumbed to that. Resilience runs in my family, and it was during those tough times that I learned how to lean into that strength. Whether it was learning to navigate military politics or handling the different personalities around me, I found that the key to survival and growth was maintaining my own personal integrity.

After my time on the USS San Jose, my next adventure took me to the USS Thomas S. Gates out of Norfolk, VA. But before I reported to my new command, I went home for a much-needed recharge and to buy a car. While at home, my mom and I discussed my new car, and in my youthful confidence, I told her I was planning to drive it all the way to Virginia. My mom, always the practical one, laughed and pointed out that I had never driven through states with snow or ice, let alone as a young and inexperienced driver.

Seeing the concern on my face, she offered to drive with me and fly back. That meant the world to me.

The drive to Virginia with my mom turned out to be more than just a road trip, it became a bonding experience. We laughed, talked, and stayed overnight at a hotel where we shared more stories and laughter. But between the jokes, I began to see my mom in a new light. She was no longer just my parent; she had become my friend and mentor. I hadn't fully realized it until that trip, but my mom had transitioned from stern yet loving parent filling the role of both mother and father. This realization I tucked away into my "pocket" for the day I would have children of my own and for the day my young leaders would grow and "leave the nest."

Once we arrived in Virginia, I took my mom to the airport to drop my road buddy off and she hugged me and kissed me on the cheek and said, "I love you." Now it was time to check into the Navy's east coast barber school before reporting to the ship. I walked into the classroom with my orders in hand, and the instructor greeted us warmly. There were ten of us in the class, and after we settled in, she asked, "Who already knows how to cut hair?" I and three others raised our hands. There was another guy who was just learning but knew the basics. The instructor then said something that took us all by surprise: "Thank God, because I don't know how to cut hair." We laughed, thinking she was joking, but soon realized she was serious.

This was one of the many lessons I learned during my time in the Navy. Sometimes you're thrust into a situation where you don't know what you're doing, but you're expected to quickly figure it out. Our class bonded over that realization, and those of us who could cut hair took it upon ourselves to teach the others, including our instructor. It was a humbling experience for all of us, and it taught me the value of grace in leadership. Sometimes, admitting you don't know something is the first step toward becoming a better leader. Our instructor's humility in accepting help allowed us to grow together as a team.

Grace goes a long way when you approach life with humility. Our instructor could have easily put up a front, pretending she knew more than she did, but instead, she was open about her limitations. That vulnerability made her a better leader in our eyes and created an environment where we felt safe to learn and make mistakes. It was a powerful lesson in humility, and it reminded me of a couple verses in the Bible that say, "The one who has knowledge uses words with restraint, and whoever has understanding is even-tempered. Even fools are thought wise if they keep silent and discerning if they hold their tongue." Leadership isn't always about having all the answers; sometimes, it's about knowing when to listen and learn from those around you.

In life, we're not always going to be the smartest person in the room. But if we're humble and observant, it doesn't take long to figure out who is. I've never advanced through life and in my career because I was the smartest or most eloquent, but I did understand people and teamwork. I understood that if I surrounded myself with people smarter than me, but just as humble, then we could all succeed.

As I continued my journey in the Navy, I carried that lesson with me. Grace, humility, and the ability to learn from others became pillars of my leadership style. I realized that even in positions of authority, there's always something new to learn. And sometimes, the best lessons come from the people you're supposed to be leading. But to fully grasp such a lesson one would have to place arrogance and the thoughts that you know it all to the side. Change doesn't really become change until you first embrace the thought of change and change.

Grace is something that leaders extend to their teams, especially when training and mentoring. Not everyone learns at the same pace or has the same level of knowledge, but as a leader, it's your responsibility to bring the team along at the speed of the slowest member. That way, everyone benefits. The stronger team members can step up and practice leadership by helping those who are still learning, creating a collaborative environment where everyone grows together. This philosophy is predicated on the thought of a fist. A closed fist is stronger and provides more protection and impact than an open hand.

I've applied this philosophy throughout my career. Whether I was training both senior and junior Sailors or working with my peers, I always kept in mind that we're only as strong as our weakest link. Bringing everyone up to speed isn't just a matter of efficiency; it's about building a team where each person feels valued, supported and seen. This mindset helped me become a more effective leader and solidified my belief that leadership isn't about exerting power, it's about giving up your "power" to empower others.

When people feel like you genuinely believe in them, you'll see them flourish. Pouring into an organization's most valuable asset, its people are crucial for its success. Leadership is not just about managing tasks or processes; it's about developing the individuals within the organization too. When you take the time to invest in people, they respond by giving their best, which in turn pushes the organization forward.

This principle applies universally, whether you're running a sports team, a small business, or a Fortune 500 corporation. The common denominator in any successful organization is its people. Learning to be a great leader who empowers and supports others is the key to unlocking the full potential of your team. When people feel supported and seen, they bring more creativity, energy, and passion to their work.

Throughout my Naval career, I saw firsthand how people would push not only themselves but also their leaders toward success. Your team can be the catalyst for your own promotions and accomplishments. By cultivating a culture of trust and empowerment, you create an environment where people feel motivated to go above and beyond. And when your team thrives, so do you. The mentality of "When one wins, we all win" should be the goal for teams. Looking at most professional sports teams proves this very point. Everyone may focus on the star player, but when he or she shares the spotlight, the entire team hoists the trophy in victory.

I've often been asked how I accomplished various projects or how I managed to rise through the ranks. My answer is always the same: it's not just about my individual efforts but about the grace I extended to those I was fortunate enough to lead. Providing that grace allows people the space to grow, learn, and even make mistakes. In return, they pushed me further than I could have gone alone.

I would often say, "I'm very good with failure." Meaning that if an individual that is part of the team learns from a mistake, then we all get better from it. I will gladly stand before leadership and accept all the blame and consequences. However, that's only if it was an honest mistake.

In the end, leadership is about people. When you pour into them, they pour back into you and the organization. Don't be afraid to be transparent when appropriate because sometimes you need to be seen as human, not like a superhero. A leader's success is built on the success of their super team. By believing in them, showing grace, and empowering them to grow, you'll find that they will not only achieve great things, but they will elevate you and the entire organization to new heights. Kind of like the old cartoon the Super Friends. Superman had an entire team of superheroes, and they were a formidable force together. They were great in their own rights individually, but as a fist they struck mighty blows.

When I finally arrived at my second ship, I met my supervisor, who introduced me to the team. I remember feeling a bit apprehensive, perhaps even suspicious of him because of everything I had experienced on my first ship. I didn't speak much to him and kept him at arm's length, even though I was exceptional at my job. The truth was, I didn't trust him, and it had nothing to do with his behavior. It was simply because he shared the same skin tone as those who had made my life difficult at my previous command.

One day, it was just the two of us in the office. Out of nowhere, he looked at me and said words I would never forget: "McGinnis, I don't know what happened at your first command, but we didn't do it to you." His words took me by surprise. I didn't want to acknowledge them, so I responded with a snarky, "Sure. Ok," before abruptly leaving the room. It was my way of brushing off the conversation, not ready to face the truth of what he was saying.

Later that day, I found myself lying in my bunk, unable to sleep. His words echoed in my mind. He was right. He hadn't wronged me, and he didn't deserve to be met with the distrust I had carried from my past experiences. What struck me more than his words, though, was the grace he had shown me in that moment. He could have judged me or written me off for my coldness toward him, but instead, he chose to speak up with understanding and compassion.

That moment something shifted inside me. It made me realize that grace, when extended even in the smallest ways, has the power to open doors to healing and growth. It was a powerful reminder that not all leadership comes through direct orders or force; sometimes it's in the quiet, personal moments that the biggest impacts are made.

From that day forward, I began to reassess how I interacted with others and how I carried my past experiences into new environments. His grace toward me became a lesson I would carry with me throughout the rest of my career: Grace can be a powerful leadership tool. Giving a person a fresh start or clean slate can reinvigorate them and spark positive energy into your team. Leadership isn't just about being in charge; it's about showing understanding, patience, and offering people the space to grow and heal.

What are you extending to others? Is it grace? Patience? Or are you extending a sword? I chose grace and patience.

Chapter 6: Leadership Comes With Challenges

I've been blessed to have had leadership opportunities for the majority of my life, starting way back on my first ship where I led several maintenance teams. But on the USS *Thomas S. Gates*, the dynamics shifted when I was placed in a supervisory role over my friends. This type of situation can present all kinds of challenges. When you're suddenly the boss of people you used to work side-by-side with, and then go out and have a couple drinks after work. This can give room for the potential for tension or misunderstandings. However, I found that being upfront and having an open conversation before any official decisions were made helped mitigate any potential drama. We all got on the same page early, which set a strong foundation.

In my case, I took the time to sit down with my friends and told them that I fully expected our supervisors to assign me tasks that could put a strain on our personal relationships. I knew they would test the limits to see if I could maintain professionalism while still being fair to my friends. But because we discussed this upfront, we agreed not to let any of that affect our working relationship. Communication was key, and because we handled it ahead of time, we were good to go when the challenges came. We would even laugh about it once work was over. I'm not naive enough to not understand that all this is based off maturity levels and knowing if you're dealing with a true friend because all that plays a factor.

Leadership, especially in the military, presents unique challenges when you don't prepare. I've seen firsthand how a lack of preparation can lead to confusion, miscommunication, and poor outcomes. Coming to a leadership role ready to give and receive information is crucial. But there's also a fine balance, you don't want to over-prepare to the point of saturating your team with too much information. Overloading people can be just as ineffective as not preparing enough. This is definitely a skill that is learned over time, so don't beat yourself up if you don't get it right the first time, but I would recommend looking at how those you deem successful conduct their meetings and take some things from them to implement into your leadership style.

One particular challenge I faced as a new leader was dealing with people who were older or felt they had more experience than I did. When someone feels they've "been there, done that," they can sometimes undermine your authority, either intentionally or unintentionally. Whenever I encountered this, I would bring that person into my "office" for a one-on-one discussion. I wanted to understand where they were coming from and see if we could address any concerns or misconceptions directly. Most of the time, these conversations worked, but if we couldn't resolve the issue, I'd bring in a neutral third party, someone outside of our chain of command, to mediate. If all else failed, I would escalate it to higher leadership. I always tried my very best to resolve issues at the lowest level possible to avoid passing things up the chain unnecessarily. Handling things internally kept my team cohesive and maintained a sense of ownership over our challenges. Plus, it gave the team the opportunity to see that we could work through problems without needing higher intervention unless it was absolutely necessary. It's also important to assess whether someone you perceive as negative is truly negative, or if it's simply a personal dislike. If it's the latter, that's okay as long as you address it through a conversation. In the military, you'll inevitably work with people you may not personally like over the course of your service, but it's not about your preferences; it's about the success of the team. In a corporate setting you may encounter a person you don't truly respect personally or professionally, but it's incumbent upon you to maintain professionalism and treat everyone fairly.

These approaches earned me a lot of respect from both my team and my executive leadership. They knew that if I was bringing an issue to them, it wasn't something minor. It had to be serious enough that I had exhausted all other options. Because of this, my leadership gave me a lot of grace and the freedom to run things in a way that worked for me. They trusted me to make decisions that were in the best interest of the team and the mission. That trust wasn't something I took lightly. It meant I had the responsibility to act fairly and with integrity, but it also allowed me to build a strong, independent team. My team knew I had their back, and in return, they had mine. This mutual respect created an environment where we could address issues quickly, work together efficiently, and succeed without needing constant oversight from above.

In leadership, being able to handle issues at the lowest level is crucial. It fosters accountability within the team and prevents unnecessary escalation, which can often complicate simple problems. When you manage issues directly, you also send a clear message that you're capable of leading effectively and decisively. It's about striking a balance between grace and authority. Giving your team space to grow and make mistakes builds trust, but know that you should first lay down clear boundaries. That's not to say they can't be allowed to legally operate in the gray area, but they need to know their boundaries. Their "right, left limits." This is another key to building trust and ensuring long-term success for any leader.

In the most extreme cases, if the situation didn't improve despite all efforts, the individual would be removed from the team. Leadership is about solving problems and maintaining cohesion, but it's also about knowing when to make tough decisions for the greater good of the team. Not every issue can be resolved with a conversation, and sometimes it's necessary to remove a negative influence for the sake of everyone else. Don't allow negativity to fester around your team because you could potentially lose your entire team, but it cannot be overstated that this is after a few conversations.

Another tactic I found helpful, particularly with difficult team members, was to give them specific tasks, lay out exactly how I expected them to be accomplished, and then walk away. This approach allowed me to maintain my authority while giving them the space to execute without constant oversight. It's hard for someone to challenge your leadership when they know you're trusting them to do the job, but you've also set clear expectations. I used this approach several times throughout my career. On one occasion, I was in charge of another Sailor who was the same rank as me. He didn't appreciate the task I assigned him or the deadline I set, but I stuck to the method I mentioned earlier and walked away. He ended up completing the task, and when he did, I thanked him. It clearly caught him off guard.

Sometimes, though, you encounter individuals who simply refuse to cooperate, no matter how much leeway you give them. In those rare cases, I've had to hold what I call a "one-way conversation." These conversations are exactly what they sound like, there's no back-and-forth. From the outset,

I would tell the person, "This is going to be a one-way conversation. I'm telling you what needs to be done, and I expect it to be followed." There's no room for debate in these situations because it's about ensuring that the team's overall mission is accomplished. At the end I usually ask, "Are we clear?"

While I believe strongly in communication and fairness, I also understand that leadership sometimes requires you to be firm and direct. You can't always be everyone's friend, and there are moments when you have to step up and make difficult decisions that may not be popular. In the military, there are times when quick, decisive action is necessary, and that's when sometimes these one-way conversations need to come into play.

I see it similarly to the many conversations I had with my mom when I was a kid. If she said something, that was the final word. Sometimes, she'd let me share my opinion, but she had her non-negotiables. Like, no more ice cream for the night. Be home before the streetlights came on in front of the house. Don't talk to her while she's on the phone. This was a big one! And, under no circumstances would I be allowed to speak disrespectfully to an adult. That last one definitely had me a little worried about my own safety.

But I digress. Balancing these two aspects of leadership, grace and firmness is an ongoing challenge. It's something I've had to refine over the years, and it's taught me a lot about the complexities of human nature. People respond to leadership in different ways. Some need more guidance, while others thrive when given autonomy. Being able to read your team and understand what each individual needs is what separates good leaders from great ones. Some people use the term "read the room." This is very true regarding your team.

When you lead with grace, people will naturally be more inclined to follow you. They'll trust that you have their best interests at heart, even when times are tough. But when you combine that grace with firmness, you create an environment where respect and accountability go hand in hand. That's the kind of leadership that earns loyalty and dedication from your team. Throughout my Naval career, I've come to realize that leadership is not just about achieving the mission, but it's more about developing people. If you invest in your team, they will invest in you.

They'll push themselves harder, rise to the challenges, and ultimately help you succeed in ways you never imagined both professionally and personally. Making the effort to understand each team member, what drives them, what shapes their character, and what motivates or discourages them, is another essential tool to use. Study them. Not in a creepy way, but study them to understand what makes them tick. What are their idiosyncrasies. This will help both you and them in the long run.

As I reflect on my experiences aboard the Thomas S. Gates, I see how much I grew as a leader during that time. I learned how to navigate tricky dynamics, manage relationships, and make tough calls. Those lessons shaped me into the leader I am today, and they continue to guide me in my career. This time in the school of Navy shipboard life emphasized to me that leadership isn't about being perfect; it's about being adaptable, approachable, and consistent. It's about building trust, setting expectations, and sometimes, yes, having those one-way conversations when necessary. It's a constant balancing act, but when done right, the rewards are immense for both the leader and the team. As I've progressed in my career, I carry these lessons with me. I've learned that leadership isn't just a title or a rank; it's a responsibility. It's about bringing out the best in others while continuing to grow and improve yourself. And that, to me, is the essence of true leadership.

What leadership challenges have you faced, and how did, or how will you overcome them?

Chapter 7: Inspiration and Motivation

When I met my bride, Monica, who also served for 12 years in the Navy, I was in a rough spot. I didn't have a car, was living in an apartment with two roommates, and was scraping by, living paycheck to paycheck. Despite that, Monica didn't just see me for who I was, but the man I had the potential to become. Plus, she knew I was pure comedy. But with all that, she didn't shy away from the challenges we faced; instead, she got down in the trenches with me, and together, we rose. Four kids and three dogs later, she's even more beautiful than the day I met her. Through every trial and triumph, outside of Jesus, she has been both my motivation and my inspiration.

Even with Monica by my side, rising through the Navy ranks wasn't easy. Every promotion was hard-earned, requiring sacrifices and constant dedication. Yet, each step forward was one of the most rewarding experiences of my life. I always say "we" achieved each new rank because Monica and I are one, and our journey through the Navy was a shared experience. Her support made every challenge manageable and every victory that much sweeter.

As I moved up through the ranks, I learned valuable life lessons at each stage. But the rank I learned the most from was during the jump from Third Class Petty Officer to Second Class Petty Officer, E-4 to E-5 for those familiar with military ranks. That period taught me the value of humility, something I hadn't fully grasped before because for over four years, I struggled to get promoted to E-5, but my reasons for wanting the promotion were wrong. I wanted to climb the ranks not to help others or better myself, but to prove to one person in particular that I was smarter, better, and more capable than he was. I was stuck on proving my worth to this individual, and it blinded me to the bigger picture. If the truth really is told, I was stuck in my mind over a person whose name I don't even remember today.

Many people remain trapped by something that happened in their past. They are still trapped by someone who hurt them or said terrible things. It's not fair, and it's definitely not right. But the truth is, that person has likely moved on and is living their life, while we're still stuck dwelling on the pain of our past. We're so focused on the darkness that we miss the brightness of what lies ahead. I could have found countless reasons why I shouldn't be where I am today, but

God's plan for me was far greater than the bitterness I held toward that person.

Now, looking back, I know it was God holding that promotion in His hand until I learned the lesson I needed to learn, humility. I didn't want the rank to be of service or to take care of my family. I wanted it purely to show this person, whose name I don't even remember now, that I could outshine him. At that point, I was selfish and arrogant, and those two traits were holding me back.

Once I understood the lesson, everything changed. I shifted my focus from proving myself to others to genuinely striving to be better for my family, for my shipmates, and for myself. After that, every promotion I earned was a testament to the hard work, sacrifices, and commitment that both I and my family had put in. From there, I climbed through the ranks, eventually becoming a Chief Warrant Officer 5, a position I could only have dreamed of when I first enlisted. The first black Warrant Officer I ever met was on my first ship. He was quiet, yet his demeanor and the way he carried himself demanded respect and invoked fear when a Sailor didn't follow his instructions.

One of the proudest moments of my career came when I was promoted to Chief Petty Officer. That promotion wasn't just about rank for me. It represented the growth I had experienced, both as a Sailor and as a person. I learned so much about leadership, responsibility, and service. Becoming a Chief meant I was now truly responsible for mentoring the next generation of Sailors, guiding them through their own challenges, just as others had guided me. This responsibility now rested squarely on my shoulders, and I embraced its gravity because I always wanted to be in positions to help people.

Leadership in the Navy, especially as a Chief, wasn't just about giving orders. It was about setting an example, showing younger Sailors what it meant to be disciplined, humble, and dedicated. I knew I had to be the kind of leader my Sailors could look up to, someone who led with integrity and inspired others to follow not because of authority but because of respect.

It was during this time that I truly understood what it meant to serve selflessly. I thought I knew before, but this was different. The focus was no longer on my personal advancement but on helping those around me grow. In my mind, if I never attained another rank, I would be okay because I was now in a position to help. But this required leading by example daily, ensuring that I not only talked about the Navy's core values but lived them out. Every decision I made, every interaction I had, was underpinned by the understanding that I was no longer just responsible for myself, I was responsible for the development and success of my entire team.

My journey from an enlisted Sailor to a Chief Warrant Officer wasn't just a story of personal success; it was a testament to the power of teamwork, dedication, and perseverance. Every rank came with its challenges, but each challenge helped shape me into the leader I eventually became. The responsibility of leadership is a heavy one, but it's also a privilege—a privilege to guide others, to help them succeed, and to watch them grow.

The lessons I learned along the way weren't just about the technical aspects of being a Sailor. They were about character, humility, respect, and the importance of lifting others up. Sometimes even pushing them past what they felt was their breaking point until they discovered they had more to give. Those lessons not only made me a better leader but also a better person.

Throughout it all, Monica was right there, by my side, sharing in the victories and helping me through the challenges. Together, we learned that leadership isn't about a single person, but it's about the team, about lifting each other up, and about being willing to make sacrifices for the greater good. These lessons didn't just apply to the Navy, but to our family. I could never have done it alone. Every step of the way, Monica and I supported each other, pushed each other to be better, and celebrated every success, no matter how small. Our journey wasn't always easy, but it was always worth it. From the late nights studying for degrees after putting our precious children to bed, to the times the Navy separated us because duty called. We've had each other, and more importantly, God had us both.

As I look back on my career, I am filled with gratitude for the lessons learned, the people we've met that have become closer than some of our own blood relatives, and the experiences that shaped me. But more than anything, I am grateful for Monica and the life we built together. She truly is my greatest gift and achievement. She is my air!

But real pause and think about this, no leader has ever achieved success without a source of inspiration. If you look through history, you'll see that something or someone always drives people to achieve their goals. Whether it's to improve their lives and their families, earn more to change their circumstances, out of anger, revenge, or simply to be recognized as "that person." Inspiration is a critical piece of leadership. Once I discovered my W.H.Y (What's Hurting You), it served as an additional catalyst to achieve my goals.

Growing up in Houston, with a love for TV shows and movies, my first inspiration was to work for NASA. I didn't dream of becoming an astronaut; instead, I wanted to solve problems. Like in the movies, when astronauts would say, "Houston, we have a problem," I wanted to be the one in Houston who'd respond, "No, you don't. I'm here to fix it." Even as a child, my focus was always on helping people. The desire to make a difference was what motivated and inspired me. That same drive to help others has followed me throughout my life and career, shaping the leader I've become.

What's your inspiration and motivation?

Chapter 8: All You Need Is A Vision

A couple of my absolute favorite movies growing up were *Pretty Woman*, *Top Gun*, and *An Officer and a Gentleman*. I still watch *Pretty Woman* and *Top Gun* once a year, but *An Officer and a Gentleman* holds a special place, and I watch it at least three times a year. Now before you laugh too hard, I loved watching Pretty Woman with my mom and since her passing I still watch it and think of those times we popped in the VHS. For me, *An Officer and a Gentleman* represented so much. It told the story of a young man who grew up in difficult circumstances, bullied, and raised in a single-parent home with little money. He eventually learned to defend himself, went off to the Navy, and found humility. He realized there were bigger things in the world than himself and that he needed to care about them. It took losing a dear friend, his girl and almost his potential career.

One of the most iconic scenes is when he finally gets it together and goes back to that plant to get his love. Right now, I can hear her friend's words: "Way to go Paula, way to go!" That scene invoked tears of joy and excitement all at once. You're reading this and I know you felt the same way so don't judge. But Paula stuck with him through all the lessons he had to learn, all the growth he had to go through. He discovered his purpose, he discovered his W.H.Y. (What's Hurting You), and she helped him realize he needed a vision. That resonated with me deeply because sometimes we need a person that's willing to challenge us to be better and get down in the mud with us to motivate us to get out.

Back in high school, my friends and I dreamed big. We raised money, scraped together change, and paid for studio time because we wanted to become a famous singing group. We performed in school talent shows and recorded tracks. One day, we even auditioned for a record label, but they were looking for a girl group at the time. The Talent Scout said, "Y'all have a great sound, and I'll keep you in mind," but deep down, we knew it wasn't happening right then. Looking back, I realized what was missing: vision. We had all the passion in the world, but no clear vision.

Vision can't just be about wanting a big house or lots of money. That only motivates someone for so long. Our group had different backgrounds, with some of us coming from upper-middle-class homes and others from more humble beginnings. We all had different ideas about what success looked like. And that's okay, but it wasn't a recipe for group success. The key wasn't that we all had to have the same exact vision, but we needed to at least be rowing in the same direction if we wanted to succeed.

The Bible says, "Where there is no vision, the people perish." Vision is that important! It gives us direction and purpose. When I was stationed in Norfolk, I realized my job had very little upward mobility. So, after talking to my Bride, Monica, and some mentors, I decided to make a change. I had to pick something I'd enjoy and something that offered a future both in and outside the Navy. Once I had that vision, my entire approach to life shifted. I became laser focused. Whatever obstacles that were in my way I either moved, climbed over, ran through, or blew up. Nothing was going to deter me from bringing the vision to fruition. After I completed all the required schooling for my new career path, I didn't stop studying. I had a vision, and I refused to let up until I achieved my ultimate goal. That goal wasn't just about becoming an officer; it was about reaching the rare and highly coveted rank of Chief Warrant Officer 5. This rank is so rare that those who achieve it are called

"Unicorns." But it all started with a vision I formed back in 2006, and I never lost sight of it.

I shared my vision with my family because I needed them to be with me on this journey. When times got hard, they prayed with me and for me, and they held me accountable. I knew what this vision meant not just for me, but for them and for the people I could help along the way. That accountability kept me grounded and focused. Vision doesn't just fuel your personal ambition; it impacts everyone around you. When people believe in your vision and you believe in theirs, it creates a powerful dynamic that can drive success. This is what I learned both in my personal life with Monica and in my Navy career. Achieving the rank of Chief Warrant Officer 5 was not just about personal accolades. It was about fulfilling the vision that would benefit others as well. It allowed me to help fellow Sailors, guide them in their own careers, and be a source of support for my family. We all need a village.

It was a culmination of years of hard work, persistence, and the ability to stay on the course no matter how tough things got. It was a testament to the power of having a clear vision and working relentlessly towards it. Without vision, it's easy to get lost. Whether it was chasing a music career in high school or pursuing a Navy career, having a clear purpose and direction is what made the difference.

Looking back now, I see how all the pieces fell into place. The obstacles I faced and the setbacks I encountered were all part of the process that shaped me. Each experience, whether good or bad, was a building block toward the ultimate vision I had for myself and my family. It's like having Legos. You end up using all kinds of shapes, colors, and sizes to achieve the vision in your head.

I'm grateful for my family and my Navy family, who believed in me and helped me see beyond the immediate challenges. They reminded me to keep my eyes on the bigger picture, and that's what vision is all about. It's about having a reason to keep pushing, a reason to rise above the noise, and a reason to wake up every morning with purpose. Without that, I wouldn't have achieved half of what I have. Vision is everything, and history is filled with examples of people who changed the world because they held onto a powerful vision. Benjamin Banneker, for instance, is not widely celebrated enough for his remarkable contributions. He was a self-taught African American mathematician and surveyor who created the plans for Washington, D.C. His vision of a thriving city where the seat of government could be established shaped the nation's capital. Without that vision, the city we know today might look very different. Where would our nation's capital even be? Vision is critical to success in any area we want to achieve success in.

Harriet Tubman's life is a testament to the strength of vision. She envisioned not only her own freedom but the freedom of her people, and she never wavered from that goal. Despite the dangers and the obstacles in her path, she made that vision a reality by leading countless enslaved people to freedom. It was her vision that kept her moving forward, even when the odds seemed insurmountable.

Dr. Martin Luther King Jr. is another example of the power of vision. The Bible tells us to write the vision and make it plain. His dream of racial equality in America led him through marches, jail cells, and countless acts of resistance. His vision of a society where people are judged by the content of their character rather than the color of their skin is still a guiding light for justice and civil rights movements today. He knew that without vision, progress would be impossible to achieve.

Samuel Morse also revolutionized the world with his vision. He saw a future where information could travel faster than ever before, and from that vision, he developed the electronic telegraph. The telegraph not only transformed communication but paved the way for the technology we rely on today. His vision connected the world in ways previously unimaginable, demonstrating how innovation starts with a single idea.

Henry Ford, with his vision of affordable, mass-produced cars, forever changed how people move. His vision went beyond just creating a faster mode of transportation; it was about making it accessible to the average person. The automobile revolutionized industry, society, and culture, and Ford's vision played a pivotal role in shaping the modern world. These individuals demonstrate that vision doesn't just change lives; it changes history.

The world of transportation would be utter chaos without Garrett Morgan, the brilliant inventor who created the three-position traffic signal. His innovation improved road safety by introducing a warning light between "stop" and "go," preventing countless accidents and revolutionizing traffic management. Morgan's vision and ingenuity transformed how we navigate streets, shaping the modern transportation system we rely on today.

We celebrate and honor individuals with vision because they revolutionize the world. Yet, in most cases, they began with the simple goal of making things a little better than they found them.

What's your vision? Write it and make it plain.

Chapter 9: The Importance of Community

Community is all I knew growing up. Even before I truly understood the meaning of the word, the feeling it gives and the role it plays, was already deeply ingrained in me, and placed there by my family. It was part of my everyday life, an unseen thread weaving through the neighborhoods I walked in and the people I encountered.

Walking the streets of the 44, specifically West D, the community was thick. We all knew each other in some way, whether through family, school, or just by being neighbors living on the same 1.5-mile street broken into 3 parts. Even the "thugs" had a sense of responsibility toward us younger kids, especially the ones they felt had a future worth protecting. They wouldn't allow us to get involved in drugs or hang around anything that would bring trouble to us or our parents. If we tried, they would give us a stern warning, but it was clear that they didn't want to see us going down the wrong path.

I grew up navigating two very different lifestyles, and for the most part, my mom never knew the full extent of it of the other. Now wait. I'm not saying I was out doing nefarious things, but because of how the street was designed, we would all in some way see, hear, or be involved with something that our parents nor the police would approve of. My mom worked long hours to support us, and I didn't want to add to her worries because she had enough on her plate. Even though my friends and I were exposed to both sides of the street, I always had a sense of responsibility. I didn't want to be another burden to my mom, especially given the struggles she faced as a black single parent in her white male dominated world.

Throughout my career, I never forgot where I came from. The community in Acres Homes helped to shape who I would become, and I carry those lessons with me every day. Even in the Navy, I found another type of community, one built on shared experiences, challenges, and triumphs. It is a brotherhood and sisterhood, forged from laughter, blood, sweat, and tears. The importance of community was something that I had learned early on, and it was a value I worked hard to foster wherever I was stationed. I wanted our children to have a small taste of what I learned and felt from my community growing up. Minus the bad things.

In the Navy, I made it a point to get involved in community outreach programs, both on and off base. Whether it was organizing events for the families of deployed Sailors or volunteering at local schools, I wanted to give back to the community that had supported me and our family. I knew how much a strong community could change lives, and I wanted to be a part of that change for others. Community wasn't just a word; it was about support, about lifting each other up, and that's something I believed in wholeheartedly. Those values have taken a very different turn over the years, but the foundation and essence of the definition are still there.

Key contributors to the community back home were our local churches, Greek letter organizations, and those who had a heart for service. I grew up seeing how these entities played a vital role in creating a positive impact, not just within the neighborhood but for families in need. I've always believed in the power of unity and service. I've seen how the community banned together when tragedy struck.

There was a young man who used to walk up and down West D when we were kids. We all called him Danny Boy. He wasn't a danger to anyone. Back then, we'd say he was a little "touched," but Danny Boy was always kind to us kids. One evening, we saw police cars, and there he was, in the back of one. He was thrashing around, yelling, and to me, he looked like an animal trapped in a cage, desperate for freedom. He was in such a frenzy that the windows of the police car had fogged up. Our parents, along with his, were asking what was happening and why they had him in custody. As kids, we noticed things, but we didn't always get the full story. The next day, we got the heartbreaking news that Danny Boy had died in his jail cell, alone.

The community was outraged, and the anger only grew when his family saw the bruises on his face and body. No one, except those officers and God, knows what truly happened to Danny Boy that night. For us kids, it left a void. We missed running or riding our bikes up and down the street, shouting, "What's up, Danny Boy!" Sometimes he would wave, but mostly, he just kept walking. What I learned from Danny Boy is that sometimes, no matter what life throws at you, you have to keep putting one foot in front of the other and just keep walking.

There was a time while we were stationed in Japan that we and our church family, walked door to door, introducing ourselves and handing out homemade gift baskets. It wasn't just about giving gifts, though. It was about reaching out and letting people know that they weren't forgotten; that someone cared. These small acts of kindness brought the community closer together. Seeing the smiles on people's faces after we'd visited their homes was incredibly rewarding. Some of the people we visited were initially hesitant to open their doors, but over time they did, and a few of them came to church. That was the ultimate reward for me, seeing that our small acts of service helped to change lives. It was a reminder that even the smallest gesture can have a lasting ripple effect, creating positive change.

Back then, even though we were in the military, we weren't rich by any stretch of the imagination, but that didn't matter. The value of community wasn't in the material things; it was in the way we supported and uplifted one another. I carry that lesson with me, both in my personal life and in my professional life.

My community in the 44 taught me the importance of resilience. Most of the people there weren't rich monetarily, but they were rich in spirit, love, and the will to help each other. It was a place where despite the occasional chaos, the sense of community could be felt. It wasn't about what you had; it was about who you were and how you played your role and contributed to the greater good. Sure, having things played on the minds of some, but for the vast majority, these weren't the prevailing thoughts. But the sense of unity and responsibility was something I took with me into my Navy career. Even though the Navy is a larger institution, it still mirrored the sense of community I grew up with. I was in a position where I could give back and be a part of something bigger than myself, just like I had seen back home. In every leadership role I took on, I always aimed to create that same sense of community that I had grown up with. I wanted my team to feel supported, not just as employees or Sailors, but as people. A strong community can create the foundation for success, and I made it my mission to foster that wherever I went because when we create a sense of community in our workplaces or our lives, we create a space where people can thrive. I learned that lesson early in life, and it was something I held close to me in the Navy. When people feel like they're a part of something, when they feel supported, they will do more, they will give more, and they and everyone around them have a true chance at achieving success.

In the Navy I learned how to build a different kind of community, one that wasn't just about shared geography but about shared purpose. I found that if the team centered our thoughts on a common goal, theme, or enemy, then that banned us together. I found that no matter where I was, if I invested in my team, my newfound family, if I built a foundation of trust and support, I could create a community that could accomplish great things. Through this I was able to experience the power of community on a larger scale. The bond I formed with fellow Sailors wasn't just about working together; it was about building a network of support that helped each of us grow. Whether we were deployed or stationed on shore together, we learned that we were stronger together.

No matter where I went, whether it was Houston, Norfolk or overseas, I made it a point to be involved in my local community. From volunteering at schools, coaching youth sports, or mentoring young Sailors, I always tried to make a positive impact wherever I could. I knew firsthand how much it meant when someone gives back. One of the most rewarding aspects of my career was seeing how I was able to contribute to building stronger communities both in the Navy and in the places I lived. I was fortunate to experience that sense of connection and support not only from my family but also from the extended families I became a part of. The church being one of the most inspiring and critical pieces of the puzzle that put together a man named Ron.

Even as I moved up in my career, I never lost sight of what that community meant to me. It was the foundation of my success and my happiness. The lessons I learned stayed with me, and they shaped the leader I became. I carried those values into every leadership role, and it became a driving force in everything I did. In the end, whether it was in the church, Acres Homes, the Navy, or in any other part of my life, community was always the key to everything. It's the support system, the foundation, and the network that allows people to succeed and thrive. Without it, we are left to navigate the challenges of life alone. But when we have community, we are never truly alone.

What was your community like growing up and how are you contributing to a community today?

Chapter 10: Who Are You When No One Is Looking?

One of the most significant lessons I learned as a teenager, on the verge of becoming a young man, came from one of my high school football coaches. He told us, "When you start practicing even when no coaches are around, just because you want to get better, then you will improve and make an impact on the team." I understood that lesson because, around the same time, I had a deeper, personal responsibility that shaped my outlook on life. I was helping my uncle, who would come to my grandmother's house while his wife was at work. Shortly after he got married, he was diagnosed with sarcoidosis on the brain. Sarcoidosis is a serious disease; it's the same condition that killed Bernie Mac, though his was in the lungs. It compromised his breathing, and when he caught pneumonia, he couldn't overcome it.

For my uncle, the disease affected his brain, and he would experience seizures and other complications. This man was the same uncle who put a basketball in my tiny hands and taught me the game when I was a kid. Now, my coach and mentor needed me. He was still super sharp mentally, but if you really knew him you knew he lost a step, but I'd sit with him for hours, talking and keeping him company while everyone else was out. Even when they were home, I was there to make sure he was okay. I'd help him during his episodes, making sure he was safe and cleaning him up afterwards. I was 16 years old at the time, but age means nothing when it comes to showing up for family. Most teenagers would have wanted to be anywhere but there in those moments, but I embraced it, and through that, I learned so much about responsibility and care. I learned what sacrifice looked like in real time.

Caring for my uncle taught me that the work you put in when no one is watching is what truly builds character. It's easy to show up when there's applause or praise waiting at the end, but it's the quiet, unseen efforts that define who we really are. Helping him wasn't about recognition. It wasn't for a thank you or a pat on the back. It was about doing what needed to be done because it was the right thing to do. That's something I've carried with me in all aspects of my life, whether it's as a husband, as a father, or in my career.

The willingness to do the hard things, the necessary things, without needing validation, is what separates true dedication from superficial effort. There's a unique clarity that comes from self-reflection, especially in moments of challenge. When I was sitting there with my uncle, I began to understand the importance of looking inward and asking myself, "Why am I doing this?" It's a question that's relevant to every part of life. Are we doing something to be seen, for an award, for praise, or is there a deeper reason? Understanding the motivation behind our actions is crucial because it helps us grow into more authentic, emotionally intelligent individuals.

Emotional intelligence is one of the most important journeys any person can embark on. It's about understanding not just what you do, but the why that's driving it. In my case, taking care of my uncle wasn't just about being a good nephew. It was about learning what it means to truly serve and support someone you care about. There was no audience, no trophy, just me and him. That experience shaped my understanding of what it means to show up for others, and it reinforced the idea that when we give, we should give from the heart. Emotional intelligence also extends to how we engage with others. If we can't have an honest conversation with ourselves about why we're doing something, how can we expect to have an intelligent conversation with others?

Understanding your motives, your strengths, your weaknesses, and your intentions allows you to approach every relationship and task with true authenticity. When you know whose, you are, who you are and why you're doing what you're doing, you become an asset to any team, family, or community.

Through my journey, I've learned that leadership starts with understanding yourself. It's not about telling others what to do; it's about setting an example and making sure your actions align with your values. My uncle's situation was a real-life test of those values. I didn't realize it then, but looking back, it was one of the first times I stepped into the role of a servant leader, not in title but in action. Showing up for him was leadership in its purest form, and by leading with empathy, patience, and consistency.

As a high school athlete, football was one of my loves, but I realized that even on the field, the lessons I learned from helping my uncle applied. Football is a team sport, but the real preparation is often done alone. It's easy to perform when everyone's watching during a game, but what about those early morning runs or the extra reps in the gym when no one's there to see? That's where champions are made. It's in the hours when no one's watching, and you're pushing yourself because you know it'll pay off later. My coach's words about practicing on your own and my experience with my uncle taught me the same thing: effort behind the scenes is what truly makes the difference. Whether you're on the football field or in life, the real work happens when no one's watching. Success, in any field, is the sum of countless small actions that most people never see. The hours of practice, the moments of doubt, the times when you keep going even though you don't feel like it, those are the moments that define us.

I carried that lesson into the Navy, where community and leadership were core values. The same principles of showing up, even when no one is watching, have applied to my time in the service. Whether it was on deployment or during training, the ability to push myself and do what needed to be done without external validation became second nature. That's what made me a stronger leader, both in and out of uniform because in life, we are often faced with challenges that test our resolve. The lesson I learned from my uncle is that we must always find the strength to keep moving forward, even when the path is difficult. It's not about being perfect or never making mistakes; it's about showing up, time and time again, and giving your best effort, regardless of the circumstances.

As I transitioned into adulthood, I realized that the lessons of my youth, caring for my uncle, practicing for whatever sport, and self-reflection, were all foundational to my success. These weren't isolated moments; they were interconnected pieces of a larger journey toward understanding myself and my purpose. In every stage of my life, from high school to the Navy, and even now as a husband and father, the principle of doing the work, even when no one is watching, has remained central to who I am. It's what has allowed me to push through challenges and find success, not just for myself but for those around me. True leadership isn't about titles or recognition; it's about showing up consistently, with integrity and purpose. A real leader understands that as they rise up the ranks, they need to provide clues to what success looks like and reach a hand back for whoever wants to grab it. It's like a relay race in track and field. When the baton is passed, the runner with the stick yells out to the receiving runner to let them know they're ready.

I've been blessed to witness some of the greatest athletes perform at their peak, not just in the spotlight, but in those quiet moments when no one else was watching. It's in those unseen hours, in empty gyms and quiet training facilities, where they push themselves beyond their limits. These athletes don't just rely on talent; they pour in countless hours perfecting their craft. I saw them putting in extra time, watching film, and breaking down every aspect of their sport. Their dedication to the details and constant self-evaluation is what sets them apart, driving them to be the very best version of themselves.

One of the most notable examples is the late Kobe Bryant. Kobe wasn't just a star on the court; he was a force behind the scenes. He was infamous for his grueling training regimen, sometimes practicing for hours before his teammates even arrived. He would often be the first one to show up at the gym and the last to leave. His "Mamba Mentality" was about more than just winning games; it was about a relentless pursuit of greatness. His success was the result of the tireless work he put in, long before the tip-off, long before the cameras were rolling. He understood that greatness was built in the quiet moments, away from the crowd. He understood that in order to achieve greatness, one has to relentlessly pursue it.

The same goes for artists, particularly great singers. While many may think their talent is purely natural, those who reach the top spend hours honing their vocal abilities. They warm up, practice scales, work with coaches, and continually push their voices to new heights. While others might be resting, these artists are in rehearsal, striving for perfection, making sure that their performances resonate with emotion and precision. Behind every flawless note is a level of dedication that most people never see. There is a scripture that speaks both simply and profoundly. Work as if you're working for the Lord. That means we'll come in early and stay late when no one else is simply because the results represent something bigger than us.

God Himself set an example when it comes to work and rest. In the book of Genesis, we read that God created the heavens and the earth in six days, and only on the seventh day did He rest. He didn't stop or take a break until the work was finished. That's a powerful reminder that rest is important, but it comes after the work is completed. It shows that even the divine act of creation required effort, time, and perseverance before taking a moment of reflection and rest.

This dedication to excellence is a principle we see across every field, whether it's athletics, music, or even faith. True professionals understand that there's no shortcut to success. You show up, do the work, and go home. Wake up and do it all over again. Whether you're an athlete, an artist, or working in any other capacity, the effort you put in when no one else is watching is what defines your success when everyone's eyes are on you. It's the work done in private that prepares you for the public stage. The same principle applies to life in general. Whether it's in your career, relationships, or personal growth, the time you invest in developing yourself, learning, and growing when no one's looking is crucial. It's easy to show up when it's time to perform, but the real challenge is consistently putting in the work behind the scenes. That's where character is built, and that's what leads to lasting success.

Ultimately, those who are willing to put in the extra hours, to push themselves when no one is cheering, are the ones who rise to the top. They understand that success isn't handed to them; it's earned through persistence, discipline, and a commitment to excellence, no matter how long the journey takes.

And just like I showed up for my uncle, I showed up for my family, my community, and my colleagues. Every small action adds up, and over time, that's what creates lasting impact. Whether it's helping a loved one, practicing for a game, or leading a team, the effort you put in when no one is watching is what defines your character. In the end, the most important lesson I've learned is that life isn't about waiting for recognition. It's about doing the right thing, even when no one else is around. That's what builds true success, showing up, giving your all, and knowing that every effort counts, no matter who's watching.

What or who pushes you to be the best version of yourself when no one is around?

Chapter 11: Moments of Reflection

Through my over 33 years of service to this great nation, I have gained far more than I gave. The Navy taught me countless great life lessons, many of which I didn't fully appreciate until much later. One of which was what being an adult truly looks like, taking responsibility for my actions and my words. Anyone can blame others for their failures or shortcomings, but true growth comes from owning up to your mistakes and learning from them. This lesson became a foundation for everything I've done during my time in uniform. Enlisting in the Navy was a decision that changed the course of my life. I didn't know what to expect when I walked into the recruiting office that day. If someone had told me about the adventures, the struggles, and the accomplishments that were ahead, I wouldn't have believed them. The Navy exposed me to a completely different world, one that demanded more than I had ever given before. I knew I needed a change, but I had no idea just how transformative the experience would be. I didn't take the time to think through what the possibilities of what the military could offer me. I think that's because I never really fully considered it as an option because college was always on my mind.

Boot camp was my first real taste of military discipline. It was nothing like the structure I was used to in my previous job or sports. It was harder, more intense, and it required every ounce of focus and energy I had. The physical drills, the mental challenges, and the constant pressure all tested me in ways I couldn't have ever imagined, but I definitely needed. But I quickly realized that every push was designed to break us down and build us back up stronger, sharper, and more disciplined. I'm a watcher and observer, so I would always read the room. I saw that some people really couldn't take the rigors of the overall environment.

In those early days, I learned the importance of resilience. When you're exhausted, when you think you can't give any more, that's when you learn what you're truly made of. There were moments when I wanted to quit, moments when I questioned whether I had made the right decision. But every time I pushed through, I came out stronger on the other side. That sense of resilience stayed with me throughout my career, shaping how I approached every obstacle, both in the Navy and in life.

Teamwork was another critical lesson I learned in those formative years. In the Navy, you can't succeed on your own. Everything is built on working together, relying on your shipmates, and trusting that they have your back just as you have theirs. It wasn't just about completing the task at hand—it was about building a bond with the people around you. We leaned on each other during long watches, during difficult exercises, and even during moments of personal struggle.

Humility was something the Navy instilled in me from day one. I remember the first time I had to perform a task in front of my division. The pressure was intense, and I felt every eye on me. When my Chief started barking orders, I could feel my hands shaking. But it wasn't about being perfect; it was about learning and growing under pressure. That experience taught me to take criticism in stride and use it as a tool for growth. It also taught me that no matter how much you think you know, there's always something more to learn.

As I moved through the ranks, I came to understand that leadership wasn't just about giving orders—it was about service. Being a leader meant putting the needs of my Sailors above my own, guiding them through challenges, and helping them grow. Every rank I earned came with greater responsibility, but it also came with the privilege of shaping the lives of others. I took that responsibility seriously, knowing that my actions and decisions could have a lasting impact on the people under my command.

One of the most rewarding parts of my career was mentoring younger Sailors. I saw in them the same uncertainty and ambition I had when I first joined. Helping them navigate their own challenges, encouraging them when they were down, and celebrating their successes was incredibly fulfilling. I knew that in those moments, I wasn't just shaping their careers—I was shaping their lives.

Looking back, the Navy gave me so much more than just a career. It gave me a sense of purpose, a community, and a lifetime of memories. The bonds I formed with my fellow Sailors were like no other. We went through so much together—deployments, long hours, grueling training exercises—but those shared experiences created a camaraderie that will last a lifetime. We became a family, and that's something I'll always treasure.

The challenges I faced weren't always easy. There were moments of real hardship, moments when I questioned whether I had what it took to keep going. But each of those moments was a steppingstone, pushing me further along the path to where I am today. The Navy taught me to embrace hardship, to face adversity head-on, and to use it as fuel for growth.

Through it all, I never forgot where I came from. The community that raised me in Acres Homes was always in the back of my mind. The lessons I learned growing up—the importance of hard work, integrity, and looking out for others—stayed with me throughout my career. In many ways, the values instilled in me as a child were reinforced and expanded upon during my time in the Navy.

I also made it a priority to give back to the communities I was a part of, whether it was through mentoring Sailors or participating in local outreach efforts. I knew how much a strong community could change lives, and I wanted to be a part of that change for others. Every act of service, no matter how small, was a way to pay forward the blessings I had received.

Now, as I reflect on my 33 years of service, I am filled with gratitude. I am grateful for the opportunities I had to serve my country, to travel the world, and to make a difference in the lives of others. I am grateful for the lifelong friendships I formed, for the moments of laughter and the moments of tears, and for the experiences that shaped me into the person I am today.

I am also deeply proud of what I achieved. From the day I enlisted to the day I retired; I gave my all to the Navy. I rose through the ranks, took on new challenges, and grew as both a Sailor and a person. <u>The Navy didn't just give me a career—it gave me a life of purpose and fulfillment.</u> I truly understand what President JFK meant when he said, "I can imagine no more rewarding a career. And any man who may be asked in this century what he did to make his life worthwhile, I think can respond with a good deal of pride and satisfaction: 'I served in the United States Navy.'"

Every step of the way, I had my family by my side. My Bride Monica, my kids, and even my dogs were all part of this journey. They sacrificed just as much as I did, and their support made all the difference. I couldn't have done it without them, and I am forever grateful for their unwavering love and encouragement.

Now, as I move into the next chapter of my life, I take with me the lessons I learned in the Navy. The values of resilience, teamwork, humility, and service will always be a part of who I am. And while my time in uniform has come to an end, my commitment to making a difference in the world has not.

When you reflect back over your life, what are the moments of resilience, humility, growth, and gratitude?

Chapter 12: Lessons From an Airman

The Navy gave me more than I ever expected. It gave me a sense of belonging, a sense of purpose, and a deep understanding of what it means to serve. I will always carry that with me, and I will continue to strive to live up to the ideals the Navy enhanced in me, that God, my momma and Mema placed in me.

One of the most influential people in my life, aside from God and my family, was a man named Colonel Charles Dryden. He was a Tuskegee Airman, a black American hero whose story many may not even know, but to me, he was more than just a historical figure. He was someone who saw me! Not just as a young man trying to make his way in the world, but as someone with potential, worth investing in. In me he saw a son, husband, father, and fellow serviceman that loved God. Before it was common to say someone "sees" you, Charles Dryden truly saw me. He spoke to me as if I were one of his own children, taking the time to pour wisdom into me when he didn't have to. He encouraged me, uplifted me, and shared lessons that still shape who I am today.

I met him in 2006, during what the world would later find out was the last year of his life. In that short time, he gave me gifts that weren't material but much more valuable. He shared his experiences, his thoughts, and his heart with me, imparting lessons that continue to influence me today. One of the things that struck me most was his ability to connect with me, to give without expecting anything in return. He didn't have to spend time with me, but he chose to, and because of that, I'm able to reach out and pour into others. His impact on my life was profound, and I see it as my duty to pay it forward, just as he did for me.

Charles Dryden shared with me the deep and painful lessons he learned as a Tuskegee Airman. He spoke about the Tuskegee experiment, not just the one that questioned whether Black men could fly planes, but the more horrific experiment where syphilis was deliberately given to Black Americans to study its effects on the human body. He told me about the fear and mistrust that many Black servicemen had at the time, knowing that their government was capable of such cruelty. Yet, despite these horrors, Dryden and his fellow Airmen didn't focus on themselves. They thought about the greater good, about those who were suffering and dying because of systemic racism. They were willing to sacrifice everything for a country that treated them as less than human, simply because of the color of their skin. He shared how they felt the weight of the hopes of an entire race of people which were tied to their success and how they used it as motivation.

In our conversations, Dryden reflected on the idea of a Black man becoming President of the United States. For him, growing up in his era, it seemed unimaginable. As he spoke, I remember thinking to myself, "People probably couldn't imagine a Black man flying an airplane either." Yet, there he was, living proof sitting right in front of me that change was possible. His life was a testament to perseverance and hope, even in the face of overwhelming odds. Meeting him had a cascading effect on my life, and his influence has never left me.

I got to see Charles Dryden in his later years, a man who had been through so much, but who still loved life. He was a man who, despite his age, was still passionate about making a difference in the world. Even in his final days, he believed in the ideals of freedom and democracy and was willing to lay down his life for them. The lessons he imparted to me weren't just about the past, they were about how to live, how to be a person of integrity, and how to carry the torch for the next generation, and more importantly how to be a foundation for them to stand on my shoulders.

When I first met him, Dryden was using a wheelchair and a cane, but to me, he seemed to stand seven feet tall. His physical stature didn't matter because his character was larger than life. He never boasted about his accomplishments, but the way he carried himself spoke volumes. He showed me that being a man of impact isn't about physical strength or outward appearance, but it's about what's inside. It's about being a catalyst for change and using your life to promote growth in others. Dryden embodied that in every way.

One day, during one of our many conversations, he looked at me and said, "Ron, you need to write a book." I remember laughing and asking, "What would I share about my life? You've done things for this country that I could only imagine." But Dryden responded with something that has stayed with me ever since. He told me, "The things you've already done in your life, and the things you're going to do, are worth talking about. You've had experiences that others haven't had, and you've made it from a place that many people don't make it out of. That alone is worth sharing."

His words planted a seed in me, a belief that my life, my story, could matter to someone else. He encouraged me to use my voice, not just for myself, but to help others. It wasn't about fame or recognition. It was about paying forward the lessons I'd been given. Just as Dryden poured into me, I've made it my mission to pour into others, hoping to inspire at least one person the way he inspired me.

Looking back, I realize how blessed I was to have known Charles Dryden. His legacy isn't just in the history books or in the stories of the Tuskegee Airmen. It lives on in the people he touched, in the lives he influenced. I am one of those lives, and I carry his lessons with me every day. His faith in me gave me faith in myself, and his belief that I had something valuable to share gave me the courage to speak up.

So, I share my story, not because I think it's extraordinary, but because I pray that it might touch someone else the way Charles Dryden's story touched me. If I can inspire even one person, then I will have fulfilled the mission he gave me, to be a catalyst for change, to make the world a better place in whatever way I can. That is my prayer, and it's a prayer that started with the McGinnis's that came before me and God used a man who chose to see me when no one else did in that way, to bring it to fruition.

Who is that one unsuspecting person who inspired you to do something out of your comfort zone? Have you done it yet?

About the Author

Ronald McGinnis Sr. didn't just choose a life of service—he was shaped for it. Born and raised in the inner city of Houston, Texas, he learned early that strength comes from faith, perseverance, and the people who believe in you when the world feels heavy. For Ronald, that person was his mother, whose unwavering love and prayers carried him through every trial. Her voice still echoes in his heart, even now, guiding his steps and urging him to press forward.

Answering the call to serve his country, Ronald spent thirty-three years in the United States Navy, standing watch across the globe, leading with courage, and protecting the freedoms he cherished. His service extended beyond the uniform—ministry became his second battlefield, where the mission was the soul and the weapon was compassion. Whether at sea or in the community, Ronald dedicated his life to lifting others up, believing that every person holds untapped potential waiting to be awakened.

Today, his motivation is rooted in two unshakable pillars—his family, who give his work meaning, and the drive to inspire others to reach for more than they think possible. Every life he touches and every dream he helps ignite is a living tribute to his mother's legacy. For Ronald, service isn't something you retire from—it's a calling that lasts a lifetime.

Made in the USA
Coppell, TX
11 January 2026

66280390R00075